A-Z motivational passages

The A-Z of Life
26 motivational passages and actions for a more positive life.

Susie Moore

A-Z motivational passages

First Edition – 2017 ©

Copyright Susie Moore 2017 ©

Photo: Jamaican Sunset – used with kind permission of Sarah Norton ©

All rights reserved. No part of this book may be reproduced or transmitted in any form or by any means without written permission from the author. ©

A-Z motivational passages

With Thanks.

One of the amazing things I have learnt is that projects like this are only made possible when you have people there to help.

Thank you to the Biz Mums network in South Yorkshire, an amazing set of people in business who have inspired me to reach out of my comfort zone.

To my close friends in network marketing, for your laughter and friendship and belief.

To my family – thank you for your love and support

To Tracy, Sarah, Maxine and Ruth –

A big thank you goes to Elaine Mitchell, Empowerment Coach, who helped to motivate me to get this finished.

And to Julie Hands, for her proofreading skills.

A-Z motivational passages

Have you ever woken up and wondered if there was more to life? How some people seem to breeze through things, whilst others don't?

Me too, through Network Marketing I discovered the power of personal development. I then went to a local network meeting of lovely mumpreneurs, who talked about Vlogging. (going 'live' on Facebook) So I decided to 'blog' my way through the alphabet.

From that, I have decided to put all this together with a little exercise each day. There is a blank page following each passage so that you can jot your own notes and thoughts down, there is also a place in the header for the date that you do the exercise, this will allow you to have a look back along your journey and compare how far you have gone.

I suggest that along with this, you get yourself a journal or a notebook so that you can continue your thoughts and ideas. So when you revisit the passage, and will have more space to record the infinite ideas and potential that I know you have inside.

The aim is to give you a tool in which you can use either over 26 days, 26 weeks or even 26 months. However you choose to do this, I hope you find something that will inspire you to become the best person that you can be.

To your success.

A-Z motivational passages

A-Z motivational passages

Contents

Introduction	4
A is for Attitude	8
B is for Believe	10
C is for courage	13
D is for Determination	15
E is for Embrace	17
F is for Failure	19
G is for Gratitude	21
H is for How	23
I for I'm possible	25
J is for Journey	27
K is for KISS	29
L is for Listen	32
M is for Mindset	34
N is for Now	37

A-Z motivational passages

O is for Opportunity	40
P is for Passion	43
Q is for Question	45
R is for Reaction	47
S is for Success	49
T is for Time	51
U is for Understand	55
V is for Vision	57
W is for Word	59
X is for Xylophone	61
Y is for You	63
Z Is for Zone	65
Blank note pages	71
Further resources	72

A-Z motivational passages

A is for Attitude

It is not something we are born with, but something that develops over a period of time and is the difference from being in 'a right state of mind' or 'the right state of mind.'

Recently I picked up on a TEDx talk by Neil Pasricha called the '3 a's of awesomeness' and the first A was Attitude.

The crazy thing is we all have one, all of the time and it is ever changing based on our circumstances and who we come across. My two 8 year olds have an attitude most of the time of ' I am a year 3 I can do it by myself' yet change and say' Mum can you help me?'

Our attitude can decide whether the day is good or bad.

So what is your daily attitude and how does it reflect your life and where you want to be?

A-Z motivational passages

Task - Monitor how you are feeling now and set your phone alarm for 3 different times throughout your day and make a conscious effort to check your feelings. Write this in a journal or below.

	morning	noon	evening
2/4/18	depressed	depressed	depressed

A-Z motivational passages

B is for Belief

'Whatever the mind can believe, it can be achieved'
'Napoleon Hill'

When thinking about belief this is the first quote that came to mind.

(margin note: What do I believe in?)

We all believe or have a belief in something, for many it is God or some spiritual like figure, for some it is the theory of evolution, for others it's a team or a person.

These beliefs are the core of our being and forms our attitude and our actions. The dictionary has two definitions of belief:

1) An acceptance of something without proof

2) faith, trust or confidence.

A belief that something you want to happen, will happen, even though there isn't any proof, having the confidence, faith and trust to take the necessary action for it to happen,

.

A-Z motivational passages

ABBA

Ask - The universe, God or whoever your spiritual source is

Believe - Actually believe in your heart it will happen

Belief (hold) - Act like it is already happening and keep the belief in your heart, with trust and confidence

Action - Take the steps forward and watch the opportunities find a way to you.

A-Z motivational passages

Task – Start small. Ask the spiritual source to give you something small, a cup of tea, a parking space, write down your request.

A-Z motivational passages

C is for Courage

Courage is often something we associate with heroes, with those that we see doing what society deems brave. There is another sort of courage, which happens every day in our own lives and in those around us.

The courage to say hello in the school playground, the courage to step out and expand what is comfortable and sometimes against society norms. I spent an afternoon watching my 8 year old take part in rugby. As one of 12 children and the youngest girl there she outshone the boys with her passion. After several days of a boy in her class at school, telling her that girls can't play rugby, she had the courage to go out and do it.

There are loads of examples in our everyday lives of people displaying courage. Courage is the mum losing her unborn child and choosing to share her story with others, courage is the person who decides to step into a room full of strangers, instead of being at home and courage is telling someone that you care about them.

Look around you, be kind, be gentle, and smile, because you never know how much courage it has taken a person to get to where they need to be that day.

A-Z motivational passages

Task – On the blank page, think about all the times you have taken a deep breath before you have stepped out to do something. Once you have finished, re- read them and be proud of what you have done. Refer to it whenever you need to be courageous

A-Z motivational passages

D is for Determination

Determination is one of the qualities I am proud to possess and often people confuse it with stubbornness.

Have you ever watched a child that likes the look of something, a toy or a shiny object for example, This is amazing to watch and you can see the look of determination in their eyes.

Determination is an amazing and positive quality to have. It enables you to achieve your goals and helps drives your motivation to turn all your dreams into reality.

In 2012 I watched the Olympic torch come through my village that I grew up in and an ex -service personnel, who had lost limbs during active service in a conflict, carry the torch into the village. Also last year I watched a partially sighted girl, (who I actually found out was a friend of a friend) climb Snowdon, for Children in Need.

What quality unites these two people, DETERMINATION.

A-Z motivational passages

Task – Determination is a quality which is underpinned by motivation – Write down all the things that help motivate you? Now when you need to feel motivated you will have a list.

A-Z motivational passages

E is for Embrace

Embracing is the art of accepting. Sometimes in life we need to embrace (accept) things so we can move forward

Recently I discovered that embracing (accepting) something isn't the same as agreeing.

I went to an Empowerment seminar, there were only 5 of us in the group, some people I had met and others who I hadn't. I came out 2 hours later realising that to move forward, I really needed to embrace my current situation.

So I did

Accepting life as it is, and accepting where you are currently will help you move forward in life.

Where are you in your life right now? EMBRACE what is and what has been...and take the first step in your future....

A-Z motivational passages

Task – Write down where you are today, split it into different headings and draw a line in the sand. This is the first step to moving forward.

A-Z motivational passages

F is for Failure

We generally become aware of the idea of failing at primary school, given that the current system in the UK is set up for those who meet the government standards. You will know that your child is encountering the idea of failure when they come up with **"I can't and I am no good"** This is where, as parents, positive reinforcement comes in, if like me, in the beginning, you struggle with this, remember that it takes 4 years for athletes to train for one Olympic games.

First

Attempt

In

Learning

Understand (what went wrong)

Rethink (what can I do right next time)

Exercise new plan (take action)

Continue to repeated over and over again....until the goal or outcome is at the desired level.

A-Z motivational passages

Task – Failure means you are taking action! So look at a recent event that you feel didn't go well. Review it using the method above.

So why not start today and FAIL URE way to the top!

A-Z motivational passages

G is for Gratitude.

Gratitude is the art of being thankful and having a gr(eat) at(t)itude.

It is a mindset and one that sometimes is not easy to master...however I do try...

What would your life be like? Where would you be?

Even on the bleakest of days we have things to be grateful for. Try and concentrate on the little things. As you are reading this, a point of gratitude could be.

'I am thankful that I have learnt to read.'

A-Z motivational passages

Task - So what are you thankful for in your life today? Look, feel and see around you. Write them down. To extend this, you could always write down at least three points each day and watch in amazement how much it will change your surroundings.

A-Z motivational passages

<u>H is for How</u>

When you are doing something, and working towards a goal or a dream, have you ever noticed that everywhere you go there are things that remind you of your goal?

The example everyone uses is when you fix your eyes on a certain car and you then start seeing it everywhere. This is because you RAS (Brain Receptors) have kicked in. The cars have always been there, it is just that you have shifted your focus onto the object and ABRACABRA – as if by magic, everything associated with it, is there.

A-Z motivational passages

Task – Write down a list of a few objects (e.g. yellow car) spend the next 24 hours focusing on those objects and see what happens. After that start thinking about other things you would like to achieve, see, hear or do. Just write down and focus on those things and your RAS will soon show you the opportunities you need.

A-Z motivational passages

I is for I'mpossible

Not a spelling mistake or grammatical error! I Promise!

Have you ever heard of Roger Bannister? Over 60 years ago he was the first person ever to break the four minute mile. Before he did it everyone said it was not possible.

Throughout history there are examples of people who have done things, that to many, seemed impossible.

With hard work, a positive attitude, gratitude and determination, you can accomplish the things you want to do.

A-Z motivational passages

Task – List all the things you would like to accomplish in your life. (a bit like a goal list) Using the internet and talking to friends and family find someone who has achieved that goal or something similar. Talk to them and ask them how they did it. And if no one has achieved it yet….

Go out and do it. Have fun!

A-Z motivational passages

J is for Journey

A journey is a action in which we move from one place to another (point A – point Z) and our lives are made up of several different journeys all of which are intertwined.

First there is the big journey that we embark on from birth – death. Within that, there are little journeys - our journey through childhood, and into adulthood.

The important thing is to try and enjoy the journey and where you are at each stage. You may find looking at the rest of the letters may give you help in finding where you are on your journey.

A-Z motivational passages

TASK- A journey can only begin if you know where you are going. Take a moment and try and think about your journey. Where have you come from and where do you want to go. Think of a particular area of your life or goal. Jot down some notes and enjoy the ride.

A-Z motivational passages

K is for K I S S

K I S S is not lip to lip type of kiss, (although I did read this morning that a kiss and a hug is a natural anti-depressant! So go and give someone a hug and a kiss) but for me, K I S S is another one of those ways to remind myself about how I should be living.

K – Kindness. What is Kindness? A positive type of emotion, and the first person you need to be kind to, is yourself. Without showing kindness to yourself, you will not be able to be kind to others.

I – Integrity. What do we do and how do we behave when we think no-one is looking or listening? I knew a lady who went shopping and when she got home noticed that she hadn't paid for an item and went back to pay for it. How many of us would do that? Truthfully? Every so often I am reminded of this story and it does make me think about what I might do if it had been me.

S – Simple. There is a major shift in the world at present about collecting memories and not things. Memories are experiences and feelings. I try where I can, to keep things simple and straightforward. It is not easy when there are such demanding influences from the outside world. I am teaching my children that creating memories is so much

A-Z motivational passages

better than collecting things.

S – Smile. Smiling uses less muscles than frowning does. Try this experiment as you go about your day. Take a deep breath, push your shoulders back and smile, as you are going about your day, smile at random people as you walk by. Even if they don't smile back you will make them feel   good and it will make you feel good too.

A-Z motivational passages

Task – Write down ways in which you can be kind to yourself on a daily basis. Keep your integrity in check each day, write down all the wonderful memories you have made so far in your life and have a little memory that you keep with you each day to make you smile.

A-Z motivational passages

L is for Listen

One of the favourite sayings my teachers repeated to our class was, you have 'two ears and one mouth, use them in that proportion.'

There are two types of listening that people do.
1. Listen to reply -
2. Listen to understand -

I got asked a question recently which made me think, ' Do I listen to reply or do I listen to understand.' My initial reply was, 'of course I understand what people are saying to me' and then it came to me, at that point I was listening to reply. Instead of taking time to listen to the point, I rushed ahead with my answer. 'Touche'

So do you listen to understand or is it to reply and give them an answer?

A-Z motivational passages

Task – When talking to people today give them your undivided attention, put your phone down, turn and face them and really listen to what they are saying. Use the page for any responses you notice or how people reacted to you.

<u>M is for Mindset</u>

A-Z motivational passages

Mindset is exactly what it is...it's all to do with the organ that we have in our heads, known as a brain. It is the most powerful tool that humans have. It is computer and like all computers it has a programme of operation. How this is done, I am just beginning to find out. (My two daughters are being taught coding at school, which is designing computer programmes, and I bought a 'coding for kids' book just so I can catch up with them)

Anyway, so we are born and we have a brain, all the sights, sounds and smells we encounter daily are interpreted within our brain and then we learn and grow up...Simple!

We all have a mindset, which is largely influence by those around us, our parents, peers and anyone else we encounter Everyone we meet leaves an imprint on us.

It is our own experiences in life that has the biggest impact. The good news is, that with a bit of determination, a positive attitude, gratitude and belief in ourselves we can change the impact each experience gives us. It will take time and there will be many times where you end up back where you started, or so you think.
Affirmations are a great way to develop a positive mindset – Mohammed Ali used one all his life which was 'I am the greatest'

A-Z motivational passages

Even if you don't feel like you are there now, doing one or two affirmations daily will give you the start that you need.

A-Z motivational passages

Task - So what is your mindset? To begin with have a look at how you speak to yourself, think of at least 3 affirmations you can use each day.

A-Z motivational passages

N is for Now

Yesterday is the past
Tomorrow is the future
Today is a gift
That is why it is called NOW.

(Based on a quote by Bill Keane)

Has anyone ever said to you 'why can't you just be present?' or more commonly known as ' Don't fret!'

I remember thinking, but I am not a present?

For years, I have tried to just be in the now. When I was a younger I was a constant worrier, I would get up in the morning and worry about being at school and then at school I would be thinking about what I would be doing when I get home and then at home I would be thinking about getting up tomorrow for school and...

Well that didn't stop much as an adult, when I was at university I was worrying about being single and then when I got married I would worry about having children and when the girls were little I wanted them to be grown up and.... yes you get the idea...breathe just breathe.

On a trip, on the motorway, there was a moment, a brief,

A-Z motivational passages

moment, where I was just there in the now, where I felt calm, in control and present, music playing from the IPOD through the radio, thinking about where I was on the motorway, singing along to the songs...enjoying being present, in that moment.

A-Z motivational passages

TASK – As you go about your day stop and enjoy each and every moment. Focus on where you are at that given time. Make a note of how that pause makes you feel. Bring it into your day for at least a week and notice the changes around you.

A-Z motivational passages

O is for Opportunity

What is an opportunity? Well - opportunities occur all around us every day.

When in the morning you open your eyes after a sleep you are given an opportunity, a chance to get up, you are then presented with an opportunity to eat, to put on clothes etc... another way of looking at opportunities is looking at them as possibilities.

Every moment of each day there will be some opportunity or possibilities. Today a great friend took an opportunity - a moment - to ring me and say hello.

So opportunities are moments - brief periods of time - did you know that a day is comprised of 86,164.1 seconds.

We have 86,164.1 moments (opportunities) each day and each moment is unique.

Sometimes we need to live in the moment (see N for Now) sometimes we need to be open to the opportunities around us and help others to see their opportunities. Do we take the opportunities to tell people how much we care? Sometimes opportunities pass us by and when it does and we can recognise it as a missed opportunity, it is the universe's way of communicating to us, to seek more opportunities,

A-Z motivational passages

possibilities and moments. Acknowledge the missed opportunities and keep watch for the next. If in doubt create opportunities for yourself, this is done by taking some action. The more opportunities you acknowledge (even the small ones) the more you will be presented with them.

Repeat daily 'today I will find opportunities in everything and embrace them as they flow my way'

A-Z motivational passages

Task – As you go about your day look out for the opportunities around you. Write down the opportunities you want to look for.

A-Z motivational passages

P is for Passion

True passion is a deep emotional feeling, an intense desire for something. Have you ever watched someone when they talk about something and the spark that shines?

Blessed are those people who can make a living from things they are passionate about - they never work a day in their lives

Passion is associated with being in love or having a love of something, it has been known to be a reverse negative feeling as well. Passion is igniting a fire, which is where the phrase, "burn with passion" comes from and a burning desire. Passion also comes from belief, which is why life coaches talk about having a positive mind-set.

At a time in life where many people are unfulfilled by many things, including their work, it is good to find something positive that sparks a flame!

A-Z motivational passages

Task – We all have things that we are passionate about doing. Write down all the things you are passionate about. Then go and do them.

A-Z motivational passages

Q is for Question?

A question is simply asking something, isn't it?
Sounds pretty simple? So why is asking questions so important, when it comes to our own health and well-being? What? Isn't a question asking somebody else, something, to get information from them?

Would it surprise you to know that the most questions we ask are to ourselves? and in this instance, it is the answers that are the most important, not the questions.

Problems are just questions which need an answer.

Sometimes we don't have the answers straight away.

A-Z motivational passages

Task – Write down all the 'problems' that you are facing in your life right now. Next to each problem write 'How can this be solved?' Read each problem through one at a time the answers will come, reread your list and repeat the phrase. The answers will appear because you are looking for them.

A-Z motivational passages

R is for Reaction.

You can't change what people do or say, but you can control your reaction and that is where your power lies'.

One thing I have been learning lately is that when something happens beyond your control, learning to control your emotions is key. Yes, you do need to express the emotion you are feeling, otherwise it eats away at you.

Journaling is a good way of dealing with the emotions and is a great way of ranting if you need to. This way you can;
1. Express what you need to say – without hurting anyone
2. Get everything out of your head and on to paper, giving you a clear mind to concentrate on the important things.
3. You can come back at a later day and review the situation with a degree of clarity.

It is also important to be aware that you are not responsible for other people's reactions. This is not easy, especially when you see the person as a friend (or even family.) A reaction is a person's interpretation of an event or situation and all this is governed by:
1. Their internal beliefs;
2. Their environment;
3. Other things that may be happening for them.

A-Z motivational passages

Task – become aware of how you react to people. During today when you have interactions with people, write down how you respond and how others respond back.

A-Z motivational passages

S is for Success

Success is waking up each day,
knowing as you go your way,
you are happy, true and kind,
helping others, then you'll find,
that kindness coming back to you.
Whatever you say and whatever you do
Is a true reflection of you!
Success is giving, for no reward,
Success has no time for greed or points scored.
Success is a positive, personal thing,
Success has no time, nor negative ring.
Success is something we all can share
Success is with us everywhere
Success is going to bed at night
knowing you have done things right,
knowing that in every way,
you've had an amazing successful day. © Susie Moore 2016

A-Z motivational passages

Task - We all have our own belief and thoughts on what success is. Write down all the accomplishments you have achieved over the past week and then write what success means to you.

A-Z motivational passages

T is for Time

Time is a unit or measurement we use to get from one moment to another. We have seconds, minutes, hours, days, weeks, months and years. If you are reading this in the UK we work on Greenwich Mean Time (invented by the Royal Navy years and years ago,) and the rest of the world are either hours ahead or hours behind. Sounds straight forward?

One of the most common excuses I hear is 'I don't have the time' It has been proven that the average person has enough time each week for another full time job!

We have approx. 4000 weeks in our lifetime. Each moment and day is a blessing, so this weekend I have been thanking the people around me for the things that they have done for me, living in the moment, the now. Improving my life by a doubling penny (if you want to know more about this, type '1p or a million pounds' story or the slight edge into a search engine)

Time is such a valuable commodity, yet sometimes it is not appreciated with the value and respect it deserves. Time can be your friend if you let it, time is the one thing you can spend but never earn more of, so when you give your time to someone you are giving them something precious.

So if you want to give someone something more valuable that diamonds, give them your time.

A-Z motivational passages

TASK – Spend a day monitoring your time. Use the next page to write in how you spend your time.

Are their areas where you could be working towards a goal, hobby or passion?

If you want to do this over a week then photocopy the sheet below.

A-Z motivational passages

Date and Day

Time slot	Activity

A-Z motivational passages

A-Z motivational passages

U is for Understanding

Trying to understand why things happen to other people is not important, but trying to understand who are you is.

What is important is that people try and understand who they are. I read a beautiful phrase, in a book, which goes like this:

Help me to learn the truth about myself no matter how beautiful it is. (Happiness Now – Holden R)

Understanding ourselves is the key to helping others.

A-Z motivational passages

Task – The key to understanding, is to look at what you believe. Write down everything you believe about yourself. This will help you find where you are in your life.

A-Z motivational passages

<u>V is for Vision</u>

We all have visions in our life, they are dreams, goals, or aspirations.

Take a moment in a favourite spot, sit down, take some deep breaths and picture a scene of something you would like to do.

Where is it? Who are you with? What are you doing? What sounds can you hear? What smells are around you?

If you can't easily picture or think of something go back and look at H for How where you have some of the things you would like to do.

What are the feelings associated with achieving a goal?

A-Z motivational passages

Task – If you haven't already done so, go and do H for How. Then using the above technique visualise a goal you would like to achieve. On the next page write the goal, the date and all the feelings you have visualised for yourself in achieving the goal. Repeat as often as you need to…

A-Z motivational passages

W is for words

Words are powerful; an anagram of words is sword. A sword can either raise your status (being knighted) or bring you down (and in some instances, kill)

Words are used every day, (you are reading them now!) we speak to others, we write things down and we speak to ourselves.

What do you say to yourself? What are your thoughts?

A-Z motivational passages

Task – I would like you to become more aware of your thoughts. During the day monitor your thoughts. Are you being kind to yourself? Are you saying positive or negative things to yourself? How do the things you say make you feel? Write down what you are saying. Go back and have a look at the M for Mindset. Can you use the task there to help improve and change any negative thoughts to positive ones.

A-Z motivational passages

<u>X is for Xylophone</u>

Xylophone is a musical instrument and is one of my favourites. In the A-Z the Xylophone represents how much music plays a part in people's lives and how it is a great tool for helping you feel motivated and happy.

Music can provoke memories, both happy and sad. I used to play the type of music that reflected the mood that I was in, now I play music to reflect the mood I want to be in.

A-Z motivational passages

Task – play a piece of your favourite music and see how you feel when you play it. Do the same with another. Write these names/titles down with the feelings associated with them. Then you will have a reference to the types of music you need to play when you want to be in that mood.

A-Z motivational passages

Y is for You

YOU are the most important person in your life!

With children, parents, family and friends needing our time, this is the hardest thing to grasp.

It is ok to choose what you do and don't do and you can give yourself permission to make any decision without feeling any guilt.

Taking time out for you to rest and enjoy doing things is one of the greatest gifts that you can give yourself

A-Z motivational passages

Task - Write down all the things you enjoy doing to relax. It could be sitting outside, with your favourite drink, going for a walk, listening to a piece of music.
Find at least 5 – 10 minutes in your day to implement one of these activities, enjoying and living in that moment.

A-Z motivational passages

Z is for Zones

"Life begins at the end of your comfort zone"
Allan and Barbara Pease"

We are all guilty of getting into routines, going the same way to work or sitting in the same seat...and this is where we become comfortable. This is good and does help us. To grow and develop more, we need to occasionally do things different.

A-Z motivational passages

Task – Start with being aware of your daily routine, do you go the same way to work each day? Do you sit in the same seat? Do you do the same thing at lunchtime? Write you daily routine down. (I have added another time sheet on the next page and a blank page)

Now think about ways you can slightly change things. Can you go an alternative route to work? Sit in another seat?

Note your feelings.

Can you think of other things?

A-Z motivational passages

Date and Day

Time slot	Activity

A-Z motivational passages

A-Z motivational passages

A-Z motivational passages

Congratulations – you have reached the end of alphabet – however this is just the beginning of an amazing journey. Keep using the book, and tell others about it.

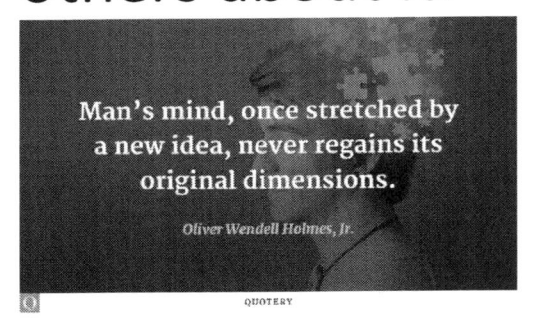

> Man's mind, once stretched by a new idea, never regains its original dimensions.
>
> Oliver Wendell Holmes, Jr.

A-Z motivational passages

For your notes....

A-Z motivational passages

Further resources

This page shows some of the resources you can use to continue your journey of personal development.

Referenced in the book

Elaine Mitchell – Empowered Souls
Robert Holden – Happiness Now
Barbara and Allan Pease – The Answer (audio cd)
TED X talk – the 3 a's – www.ted.com/talks
Jeff Olsen – The Slight Edge
Darren Hardy – The compound effect

A-Z motivational passages

Printed in Great Britain
by Amazon